NOT

MW01609574

MY UNDERPANTS

Diane Gunlogson

Editor: Kathleen Trombley

Front Cover and Opening Picture: Stephanie Thate

Illustrations: Karen Guay & Andrew Dominski

Back Cover Photo: Christina Davis

Printed By: DiggyPOD

ACKNOWLEDGEMENTS

I would like to thank my family, friends, and friends I didn't even know I had for all of their prayers, thoughts, cards and support to pull me through the scariest time of my life. I suffered a ruptured brain aneurysm on April 24th, 2009 and this story is really a synopsis of the funny, touching, interesting events that occurred from the time shortly after the aneurysm burst until today.

I began writing this book as a form of therapy. I knew I would have it done in a year. It is four years since I wrote my first words. I would awaken each day and say I am going to write for several hours. I would eat breakfast and the next thing you know I was still drinking my tea at noon. Don't remember what I was doing or why. Besides the therapy for me hopefully this book will make people more aware of warning signs that they should not ignore. This would mean everything to me as maybe I can help prevent someone from enduring what I have. I was one of those: stubborn, everything is fine, I am just overstressed people. When I suffered the terrible pain in my head and neck I wrote it off as just stress.

I have also become more aware of children riding bicycles or adults on motorcycles without helmets. If they only realized that in one fall their life could be forever changed. Most people picture if they fall they might have scrapes, cuts and bruises and they will heal quickly. They do not picture their brain being injured. We need to make people more aware of brain injuries and how to prevent them. I have made many friends whose lives have been forever changed after suffering a Traumatic Brain Injury. We also have many brave men and women returning from their mission overseas with traumatic brain injuries.

I dedicate this book to my dear mother, Myrtle. She was a strong, loving, brave woman with a love of life and she possessed many hidden talents. After raising seven children she became my father's caregiver. She became so engrossed in the day to day care of him that she ignored her own health. In February of 2007 Mom was diagnosed with Stage 4 cancer. She was upbeat and stated she was going to beat this. Well my mother did fight. The Doctors told her she may have six months possibly and as Christmas approached, which was her favorite holiday; she was able to celebrate with her family. My mother was called by God on February 28th, of 2008.

I would also like to thank Karen and Kathy for being there for me literally every step of the way. Kathy is a very special friend who acted like I was a sister when this occurred. She constantly visited the hospital, kept my family informed, watched my dog and was my cheerleader. Life can take some strange turns and one of them was Karen reentering my life. I will explain this in the book as Karen was pivotal in my recovery and my happy life now.

For Stephanie-Sue: You did an excellent job illustrating my book's front cover and the descriptive first chapter. You captured the moments completely. Thank you for staying my special friend, it has been a long road for you and I truly hope that your drawings will open a new door for you. You taught me many things that I didn't realize until just recently. I would say the biggest lesson is to take the time to talk and listen to that stranger or loved one as you never know what role they may play in your life. Most of all learn to communicate and really listen to those you love and remember to play like Pooh.

CHAPTER 1

I will always remember this date: April 24th, 2009. I came home early from work stressed out over an incident that occurred. (I know you are not supposed to do that; I know to breathe and relax.) On my way home I stopped at Walgreens to see if my friend Kathy was working. We have been friends since the late 80's. Kathy was working so I asked her to please come over to dinner as I needed to talk with her. Kathy had to work several more hours before she could come to my house, but she would come. I was relieved with that and quickly drove home to sort everything out in my head. I arrived home and immediately began sorting through old paperwork trying to find a document I needed. Should I also say that during the two hours I waited for her to arrive I had more cigarettes than were good for me plus a couple of beers. By the time Kathy arrived I was totally wound up. She sat down and I immediately started spewing out what had occurred that morning. Kathy used to work at the same office so she understood why I was so upset. As I was talking I became more aware of a headache which was building in intensity.

In an attempt to calm down, I turned on the grill to cook some burgers. While we were waiting for it to heat up we sat on the porch and I continued the rundown of my day. I could not believe the way I had been treated and was extremely upset. As I talked more animatedly I suddenly felt flushed and my head and neck ached. I told Kathy I had to lie down. She gave me an ice pack and asked if I wanted to go the Emergency Room. Of course I said no. I was certain it was a migraine or stress headache and I only wanted to lie down. This is the last thing I remember doing that day. Kathy cooked the hamburgers and tried to have me eat one. I did not want it so she offered to cook me oatmeal or something plain to eat so she could give me some aspirin. I do not remember Kathy trying to see if I would eat soup or oatmeal. She wondered if it was more than a bad migraine and we should go to the Emergency Room. Now for those of you that know me, you know if I say I will not do something I mean just that. The pain in the back of my head, neck area was severe. Silly me for not listening to Kathy; she is so sensible. I can't even begin to describe the pain. I never told Kathy I felt like I had warm water floating in my skull. All I was focused on was the pain in the back of my head and neck. I insisted that all I wanted to do was sleep. Kathy told me she reluctantly went home hoping the aspirin she gave me would kick in so I would sleep.

The next morning my youngest sister, Ginnie called me early. She thought I sounded drunk on the phone which I would not be at 8 o' clock in the morning or anytime of the day, for that matter. She then became scared when I began rambling on that I would be late for work. Since it was a Saturday morning she became more nervous as I normally did not go to the office on a Saturday. At this point Ginnie hung up the phone and quickly called our oldest sister Elaine. I should add that most of my family lives in upstate New York. I moved to Florida in 2006 for a new career and had no family near me. When my sister Elaine started talking to me she was afraid I had suffered from a stroke as I was slurring my words. She confirmed this by asking me questions about my dog, Jalapeno who has been by my side for fourteen years. When I could not tell Elaine if I had fed Jalapeno or let her out to do her duty she knew I needed help. Elaine asked me if I would give her Kathy's phone number and she would wait on the phone until I came back. I said "Sure". After several minutes when I had not gotten back to Elaine she began yelling my name. I immediately said "Yes, what do you want?" I had never left the room to find my address book. Elaine then asked me again to get her Kathy's number ASAP. Somehow I retrieved my address book from my desk drawer and gave Elaine Kathy's number. (I still do not know how I did that.)

Elaine called Kathy and quickly asked if she could please go to my house. Kathy was planning on stopping by on her way to work to check up on me. She immediately jumped in her car and drove to my house. When she arrived she banged on the door until I answered it. She could see me standing in my living room. She said I was wandering around with shorts and a baggy T-Shirt on. Kathy came into the house and looked at me and asked me how I felt. I didn't know what she was talking about so when I answered rather oddly she grabbed my arm and said "Come on Diane, we need to go to the ER, what if you are having a stroke." I stood there and adamantly stated "NOT WITHOUT MY UNDERPANTS!" Kathy stood there shaking her head telling me that no one would care whether or not I had underwear on; in fact they would probably rip them off. I kept insisting I needed to find my underpants. Somewhere in that head of mine I remember all mothers saying that one never goes anywhere without clean underpants; so in my mind why would I leave the house without any on.

The phone then began ringing. Kathy quickly answered. It was my sister Elaine verifying that Kathy was there. Kathy told her I lived less than five minutes from the hospital so she was taking me there and would call her when she knew anything. When Kathy hung up the phone I was no longer in the living room. She found me in my bedroom staring at my dresser and yelling "Someone took my underpants, I can't find my underpants." I insisted on getting dressed more properly. Jalapeno came walking into the room and Kathy realized she had better put Jalapeno out and feed her so she told me to wait by the front door as she put Jalapeno out in the yard. As Kathy looked out the sliding glass door to the yard she stopped in her tracks. There in the backyard was a birdcage sitting on a table. Inside the cage were two squirrels trying to escape. (I can explain this and I will. A week earlier I had visited a neighbor who owns birds. I thought I was opening the cage for her big bird that cannot fly. Instead I had opened the door to the parakeet cage. The two parakeets made their escape. A few days later while sitting on my back porch I saw a blue parakeet pecking at the spilled birdseed on the ground under my feeder. I called my neighbor and she brought over a cage with their favorite bird treats. We were hoping to catch her bird but instead two squirrels found the treats too appealing. Once inside the cage door fell back down and locked them in.) Poor Kathy at this point didn't know what to think. Her friend is acting strangely, Jalapeno is running toward caged squirrels and she needed to get me to the hospital. Kathy grabbed a stick and while holding Jalapeno she tried to open the cage without getting too close. Kathy tried for several minutes to open the cage knowing she was wasting precious time. After releasing the squirrels and Jalapeno doing her duty she went back into the house. I was not by the door ready to go. She found me in my bedroom staring at my dresser yelling "I can't find my underpants!" At that point she took my arm and now was sure something more serious than a migraine was involved.

CHAPTER 2

Kathy arrived at the hospital and took me into the ER. She told the nurses she believed I had suffered from a stroke. I was slurring my words and had a terrible headache. She was told to sit with me in the waiting area. After a few minutes Kathy could not believe I had not been seen by anyone so she went to the nurse's desk. She asked if someone could please look at me; we had been there a while and this was serious. The nurse looked right at her and stated that if I had arrived in an ambulance I would have been seen already. Kathy quickly explained to her that I live right around the corner and that it was quicker to have brought me than calling an ambulance....plus I would have refused to get into an ambulance. (My stubborn streak again.) Finally the nurse came over and asked me my name. Of course I sat right up said my name and also spelled it for clarification. I was obviously not helping the situation. The nurse however could see I had a problem. My words were slurred and my mouth was drooping. They then rushed me in for a CT scan. This showed I had bled profusely in my brain from an aneurysm. The doctor told Kathy that the bleed was so bad he could not believe I had survived up to this point. My probability of surviving was less than twenty percent. Suddenly an alarm rang on the equipment I was hooked up to. A pair of nurses ran out from behind their station and joined the nurse already in the room. The doctor turned and rushed to assist. The alarms continued to sound as they suddenly flipped my bed over so my head was down and my feet were elevated. Kathy left the room and returned to the waiting area and sitting there were our friends Dick and Vicky. She told them what had occurred and that their friend may not survive. This hospital was not equipped to handle my needs so they quickly called two other hospitals to see who could assemble a team of neurologists and a neurosurgeon to close my aneurysm.

Luckily Bayfront Medical Center was able to take me. I say this because they are known for their brain trauma facility and rehab unit. So off I went in the ambulance to Bayfront with my friend Kathy and two other dear friends Dick and his wife Vicky following behind. By the time I had arrived at Bayfront I was in critical condition and they told Kathy they did not know if I would make it. After doing the necessary scans it was determined that the neurologist would attempt to insert a coil in my blood vessel to seal off the aneurysm. Unfortunately after making three attempts the last coil shot through the aneurysm and lodged in the frontal lobe of my brain. Needless to say the coil caused another stroke which totally affected my left side.

At this point in time my body crashed. My blood pressure and heart rate severely dropped so they had to focus on stabilizing me. They told Kathy, Dick and Vicky that I might not pull through and the neurosurgeon had to perform a craniotomy to clip the bleeding aneurysm. This was successful but again my body crashed. They induced a coma so my body could try to heal. The doctors told Kathy not to be shocked if I did not regain consciousness for several days. They also told Kathy and my friends that they should be prepared that I may not recognize anyone or be able to talk due to the extent of my brain trauma. Kathy called my sister Elaine and my brother John was able to secure a flight that would arrive the next day. Five days later after I regained consciousness and before Kathy had arrived Linda and Ruth from where I worked went to the nurse's station. They told the nurse they were my sisters. The nurse leaned over me and asked if I knew who these ladies were. She really didn't expect me to respond and when I looked at them and said "Yes, it is Linda and Ruth. Obviously this is not who they said they were. The nurse was furious and made them leave immediately. When Kathy, Dick and Vicky arrived shortly thereafter the nurse told them what had happened. In addition to the nurse being mad at what Linda and Ruth had done, she was astonished that I had wakened and was able to recognize them. They walked into my room and the nurse announced that I had company. I looked at them and said their names. I do not remember any of this at all and they had no expectation I would be able to do this so soon after surgery. I am truly blessed that they were able to keep me alive. I was in intensive care and acute care for a month before being transferred to the brain rehab unit. I was also totally unaware of the fact that my youngest brother John had flown down and sat by my side every day for a month.

While I was in acute care I kept telling Kathy that I was always being moved to different rooms. Of course this was not so. I also complained of severe leg pain. Kathy and my brother would ask the nurse to help me. When the nurse came to my side she would ask what was wrong with me. I told her that two Samoans were trying to drag me down a hole. Every time I was asked about my leg I insisted that was how I was hurt. Kathy and my brother would look at each other and roll their eyes. They knew I was in pain but obviously this was a fabrication on my part. The staff knew I was in pain but with the story I was telling who could take me seriously at this point. Kathy told me I was adamant about being dragged down into a hole. The drugs they were giving me were doing more than just relieving my pain. In actuality my pain was a combination of spasticity on my left side plus pain from a hip dysfunction I had.

On another day Kathy was sitting in my room with Dick and Vicky. I was complaining I was uncomfortable as I was leaning to one side in my bed. Kathy asked the nurse if she could make me more comfortable. Kathy said the nurse quickly pulled on the right side of the sheets twice and after I was no longer leaning the nurse looked at me and said "There Diane now you are straight." I shot up and stated "I have been gay for years and you can't make me straight now!" Now mind you; I kept my personal life personal so when I found out later on that I stated this in front of Dick and Vicky I felt funny I had said that. Kathy thought this was hilarious and repeated this story to me multiple times. Needless to say Dick and Vicky are the best of friends and now I can truly be myself when I am with them.

I have no memory of these occurrences so I have to be told. There is only one thing I steadfastly remember sometime after laying down with a headache. I vividly remember seeing my mother standing in front of me with a huge surprise on her face. We were standing in a beautiful green pasture with a bright blue sky. We hugged each other and she said to me "Honey, it is so good to see you again but it is not your time.......you must go back and I will see you again." I can picture this is in my mind over and over again. I realize now that God blessed me by seeing my Mother and that I must continue to fight as I had more to accomplish with my life. Our Mother died in 2008 after a very courageous battle with cancer. It is the first thing I thought of when I woke up in the Brain Rehab Unit of the hospital. Then I was trying to figure out why I was lying in a hospital bed and could not sit up. My left leg hurt and so did my left butt. Due to extremely limited visiting hours there was not anyone there to tell me what happened. When one of the nurses came in my room she told me what had happened. I had been in the Acute Care Unit for almost a whole month before being transferred to the Brain Rehab Unit. There were flowers on the window sill and a giant bag of cards. I found out later that I had received cards from dog owners I would meet when I walked my dog in the park. When I was not going to the park as usual they asked my neighbor where I was. He found out I was in the hospital and dozens of people from the park sent me cards. A funny thing is the cards were signed by their dog's name and then theirs listed.   It was funny as we all became friends without knowing names. I had also received cards and plants from clients I had worked with. It was amazing to see all of this. There was a very large bag of assorted chocolate candy brought by Leah, a Therapeutic Massage Therapist, who I had visited before. Kathy told me that Leah had visited and massaged my arms and legs while she was there.

The Brain Rehab Unit is quite a group of dedicated therapists, nurses and doctors committed to helping people who have suffered any type of Traumatic Brain Injury. When I first arrived to the Unit, I could not stand on my own. Should I tell you now that I DETEST BEDPANS, not to mention the fact that I could feel like Niagara Falls is going to pop out any minute but say the word bedpan and I switch to the Sahara Desert. I felt sorry for the aides as I am sure I was not the best patient when it came to them trying to give me the bedpan. After several days of now being cognizant of using a bedpan I became determined to walk at least to the bathroom by myself. I had top-notch physical, speech and occupational therapists working with me daily. After several days I was able to transfer from the bed to a wheelchair with help. This was great as now I was able to leave the bed, be wheeled to the bathroom and actually sit on a toilet. SUCCESS! This made me ecstatic. It has always been the simple things in life that I cared about most. I also gained a new appreciation for breakfast and realize why when you walk into a nursing home there are residents sitting in the hallway. We got up every morning and sat in our wheelchairs in the hall waiting breakfast. There is no way that the nurses and aides could keep an eye on everyone in their rooms. Since I had been trying to sneak into the bathroom I can imagine what some other patients were trying to do.

CHAPTER 3

I would like to stop here for a moment so I can share a beautiful poem my mother wrote before she died. My Mom loved to write poems, try to paint and just enjoy nature. Unfortunately she felt that she was not smart enough to write poetry so she kept it hidden. My mother raised seven children and was wise beyond her years. She taught all of her children how to love, respect others, the difference between right and wrong and to live your life the way you want. The following is Myrtle's poem:

Have you ever sat and watched the sun rise or better yet the sun set?
The brilliant reds and orange like a painter's palette as he starts his masterpiece.
Well next time you get a chance, look up in the sky and only then will you realize that a painter could never duplicate that breathless wonder; and it will never look the same again.
Tomorrow, the next day, a week, a month, it will be different, like snow falling from the sky.
Everything in nature is a priceless work of art, flowers, trees, oceans, mountains; even we humans are different and unique.
So enjoy each day and every scene as it will never be duplicated again.
Tomorrow it is something new.
Fill your memories like a warehouse and pull a scene you remembered; and live it once more, but tell yourself, tomorrow another wonder I will see.

I have noticed a beautiful side of myself since having lived through my mother's death and my own close call. I have definitely deepened my spiritual side. I look at the world through Butterfly Wings instead of Rose-Colored glasses. The last time I saw my mother before she died, she gave me a precious way to remember her. She asked me what one thing that when I saw it I would know it was her. I told her a Monarch Butterfly. She then hugged me and told me whenever I see a Monarch that it is actually her looking after me. I found life extremely difficult after losing my Mother, tears would flow easily, and little things would upset me. One day while working in my yard months after the funeral I had a large Monarch butterfly circling around me and Jalapeno. I could literally feel my face opening up into a huge smile. Since then I ensure there are milkweed plants in our yard to attract the Monarchs. For a little trivia that is the only plant the Monarch will lay her eggs on. The Monarch feeds from the nectar of the tiny flowers, lays her eggs under a leaf and in about 2 weeks the little caterpillars emerge. Karen and I actually have this on film as we brought a planter full of milkweed into our back porch. At one point we had 12 caterpillars chewing all of the leaves from the plants. One by one they crawled out of the planter and found a spot to hang and make their chrysalis. I was able to view all of the butterfly stages up close and personal. I will always remember the day the first Monarch emerged from the chrysalis. It was breathtaking to watch it unfold and hang for a while. After two hours it wobbly flew over to the orange tree and sat for a while. In the week that followed we observed the rest of the Monarchs emerging to start their new lives. It was a beautiful sight. Thank you, Mom.

CHAPTER 4

One day I was sitting in the hall looking at the other patients and marveling on injuries they had incurred. I am certain I looked sad. This one young, teenage boy had a severe head injury from being hit in the head with a brick. He looked at me and offered an extra container of juice he had on his tray.

I remember this sweet, quiet voice saying Ma'am, would you like my extra juice. I didn't really comprehend what he had said so he repeated it. I was so overwhelmed by his kindness that I accepted the juice and we began talking. He had such a positive attitude as he knew he would walk again and live a normal life. I asked him what had brought him to this hospital. He told me his story beginning with the fact that one day he was walking down the street with his girlfriend hand in hand. Suddenly these guys jumped him yelling that he could not be with this white woman. They were going to teach him a lesson. One of the men picked up a brick and proceeded to pound in on his head. That was all he remembered of that day. I was so touched and overwhelmed with his story and by the fact that here was this sweet, polite teenager that would be dealing with a brain injury for the rest of his life because of bigotry. There at that moment I knew I was truly blessed as my brain injury had occurred within my head and not caused by an accident, a beating or a fall. I knew that I was going to do whatever I should to regain my strength, leave that hospital, and start my life anew. Little did I know that my brain had changed me more than I thought.

Every day for a month I followed the same routine. Once I was out of bed and helped to the bathroom, I cleaned up while supervised and then started the daunting task of getting dressed with assistance. I could not believe how difficult it was. I would sit on the edge of the bed while the therapist helped me to remove my pajamas. I then had the daunting task of putting on underwear. I don't know why I worried so much about underwear previously as it was a pain to put on. I could not bend over very well. I could put my right foot in the hole but needed help guiding the left foot. We then had to try and stand me up holding onto the back of the wheelchair. We repeated this same routine with my shorts. As for my bra.......I needed total assistance. By the time I was dressed I felt tired and ready to go back to bed. Not allowed. After dressing I was wheeled out to the hallway where we were served our breakfast. After breakfast I started my therapy sessions. My physical therapy consisted of exercises and routines to regain leg strength and balance so I could walk. I couldn't trust my own body as it flopped around. It took quite of while of doing leg exercises laying on a table, trying to stand up while holding supports and then advancing to exercising while standing. During this time they worked my arms and eyes doing dexterity games. In one of these games the therapist used an item that looked like a Fisher Price toy made for a two year old. I sort of remember sliding colored rings along a wooden tube from one side to the other. I know I did more things with my arms and fingers but cannot recall what they were. It is amazing how quickly they taught me to walk with the assistance of a walker. After that I progressed to trying to walk down the hall with a therapist holding my shirt and I held the bar along the wall. I also had occupational therapy. They spent quite a bit of time having me perform tasks with my fingers and hands. My other therapy was my speech sessions. I do believe out of all of them this was the hardest. I had to concentrate, listen, and then repeat what was said to me. They also had me read short stories and then retell them. They challenged me with little games that tested my memory. My speech therapist, Ann, challenged me to read a magazine article every two or three days. I then had to write a recap of the article. I hated doing this homework but I loved my sessions as we would also laugh a lot which was very therapeutic as I have always loved to laugh. I was always exhausted after those sessions. As each day progressed and I was seeing the changes in me. In my mind I would go home in a few weeks and life would return to normal. Finally on June 3rd Kathy announced to my friends and family that the Doctor had given me an eight hour pass to go home and see my dog. The one stipulation was that Kathy had to come to the hospital for three hours of training to ensure she could help me with my walker and wheelchair. I was so excited and could not wait until the sixth. They gave me some special therapy classes teaching me how to get in and out of a car. As much as I struggled I succeeded so on Saturday Kathy came and took her training. When the nurse and Kathy wheeled me to Kathy's car I was as excited as a kid on Christmas morning. We drove a short distance and I was doing fine. Then Kathy got onto the highway and cars were whizzing by. This scared the daylights out of me as I could not handle all of the movement. I felt like we were out of control going over 100 miles per hour and that everything was spinning. Poor

Kathy was trying to drive in all of this traffic and I am freaking out. At the time I did not realize how distracting I was yelling to watch out, you are going to fast and I can't handle this. Our first stop was Kathy's house to pick up my Jalapeno. She was so excited to see me and I her. She jumped in the car and off we went to my house. I was so very, very happy to see my home. Vicky and Dick came over and we all had lunch outside along with my neighbor, Diane. We were having fun and laughing and then suddenly I felt overwhelmed with the noise. I am sure I started to cry as it was too much for me. Then I remembered that Kathy still had to take me back to the hospital. I did not want to go back but I had no choice. Needless to say, Kathy drove the side roads back to the hospital for me. I know she was exhausted from that day as was I.

CHAPTER 5

During this time in the hospital Kathy was visiting whenever she could. I don't know how she did this between her work schedule and the long drive to the hospital. She also had my dog Jalapeno at her house. Kathy was sending out daily emails informing my family members of my progress. Since I lived alone my family was looking into care facilities that I could enter upon my hospital discharge. I would not be able to take care of myself so this made sense to them. I was not aware of this until after I left the hospital. My brother took care of all of my personal bills and kept track of the insurance. Kathy brought me any letters or messages I had received on my home phone. She noticed that my old partner Karen had called multiple times leaving messages of concern as to where I was. She stated I had not responded to any of her emails when she had asked if I was okay. Kathy asked me if I wanted her to contact Karen and I said no as there was no reason to. She came back into my life before my Mother died and I didn't know if I wanted to continue much contact. Then one night I was lying in bed and I thought to myself "Diane, The good Lord has given you a second chance; I should answer Karen." Then next day when Kathy was visiting me I asked her to please call Karen. Kathy asked if I was certain I wanted her to do that as she thought I hadn't spoken with Karen for at least ten years. Karen was my first partner and we had been together for eight years. Karen and I had just started emailing and occasionally would talk to each other. Karen was deeply upset in 2007 when she learned my mother had cancer. Her mother passed away in 1997 from cancer. She said she had some old video tapes of our family from Christmas' and birthday parties. Karen asked if she could send them to my Mom so she could watch them. It was great for my mother as she totally laughed and enjoyed herself seeing old movies from 15-20 years ago. I explained all of this to Kathy so she knew why I wanted to contact Karen. I knew Karen would be concerned as I had not responded to any emails she had sent or some cards she had mailed. Since she hadn't heard from me in almost two months she might worry there is something wrong with me. This made Kathy burst into laughter as she looked at me saying "Well there is something wrong, Di." I explained to Kathy where she could find my address/phone book. She called Karen and told her what had occurred. Karen immediately said "I am coming down to help." Kathy told her to slow down and she would speak with me. Now mind you, Karen had no idea if I could walk how much assistance I would need for my personal needs and so on. When Kathy first asked me about Karen coming down I said no as I did not understand why she would want to do such a thing. I was also in denial regarding the help I would need. One day during therapy one of the therapists asked me if I wanted to check my emails on her computer. When we did I saw quite a few friends had emailed me wondering why I wasn't answering. I wasn't ready yet to sit there and answer them. Kathy was ecstatic that I had her call some friends as it was more proof in her mind that I was starting to function better and memories were intact. Karen and I spoke several times within the next week and I finally realized she wanted to truly help me and I would need it. So on June18th Karen flew down to my house. The therapists taught her how to help me with my walker and to get in and out of the car. I only had three more days that my insurance would cover my hospital stay so it was of great importance I was mobile enough for them to release me. Karen took me back to my house on the 21st. After almost two full months in the hospital I was home. I could not wait to see my dog, Jalapeno. When Kathy brought her home to me she was so happy to see her Mom. Though Jalapeno was excited, she instinctively knew to be careful near my walker. She is my special dog, very loving, smart and protective of me.

CHAPTER 6

Now that I was home I wanted to get back into my normal routine. Every morning before I went to work I had walked Jalapeno over to the local park. Obviously I was not going back to work and duh...I was not going to walk alone with Jalapeno over to the park. The first morning I woke in my house Karen had breakfast fixed for me and post-it notes stuck every where in the kitchen. After I ate I had a note to take my pills, then a note to feed Jalapeno, put my dishes in the sink and so on. I needed these notes and I still am amazed that she knew to do this for me. After breakfast I was embarrassed to tell her that I had used the Port a-Potty in my bedroom. I woke up and realized I did not think I would make it all the way to the bathroom. She looked at me and calmly said "The reason we put that in your room is for you to use and I expect you to do just that. I would rather you used that than you falling in the hallway heading to the bathroom." Right there she put me at ease but I have to tell you it is a strange feeling to know you are you but not the old you. So many things are different. My body, once strong and fit was weak. I cannot remember short term, get rattled easily, but look up at the sky every day with thanks. I am here, different, but here and so happy to be so. Next effort was taking a shower. I truly appreciated the person who invented the little shower stool. Karen was also pushing me to finish filling out my paperwork for Disability benefits. The hospital had started them for me. I reluctantly filled everything out with her assistance and we mailed it all in. I was told if I was lucky I would receive SSI in six months and would qualify for Medicaid. In my mind I would be working in six months so why do those. Thank God for Karen's insistence again.

I wanted to walk at the park with Jalapeno, it was something she loved and I wanted things to be normal. Karen put my walker in the car and drove us over to the park. We walked about ten minutes and returned to the car. Every day we walked trying to increase the length of time walking. We knew that once I could stay up for 30 minutes then I could walk from the house to the park and back. During this time I was also doing outpatient therapy three days a week. I was blessed that this facility used a machine called the Interactive Metronome for speech therapy. This machine made a sound like a cow bell and you had to clap your hands when you anticipated the sound. At first I hated being hooked up to this machine. I did not realize that this tool would help me with not just my speaking but also my balance for walking. In one month they had taught me to use a cane instead of a walker. Unfortunately after one month of therapies my insurance would no longer cover any visits. I also could no longer afford my insurance. I tried and tried to find some kind of assistance for my pill payments and my continued therapy with no luck. So at home I practiced my speech and cognitive therapies playing brain games on my Nintendo. I still needed therapy for my back and legs however. My Doctor put me in touch with a wonderful physical therapist named Shamsah Shidi. She owns Therapeutic Solutions and is the sole physical therapist in the office. She knew I did not have insurance so she charged me a reduced rate for therapy. I have a hip joint disorder that I had gone to therapy for years earlier. My hips are misaligned causing a ½ inch difference in my feet touching the floor. Walking shoots pain up my spine. When my left side stiffened up after the brain hemorrhage/stroke in the hospital it re aggravated the problem. When Shamsah first saw me I was bent over and not walking very good. Every week Shamsah worked with me trying to build up my muscles and inserted a small lift in my left shoe. Each week she would make the lift slightly higher until I started walking better and not feeling as much pain. Finally we reached the height of a ½ inch.

At that point I took my sneakers to a cobbler. He removed the sole and inserted ½ inch of rubber material between the bottom of the sneaker and the sole. My walking improved greatly and I stopped seeing Shamsah due to lack of money. I wanted to continue to see her for strengthening my core muscles. If I fell on the floor I could not stand back up. Talk about feeling like a beached whale. Not pretty.

CHAPTER 7

I know I said earlier that Karen had pushed me to fill out my disability forms immediately after leaving the hospital. (I know I said this because I have to keep rereading everything.) Six months after my disability I received my first check from SSI. (Social Security Income) This automatically qualified me for Medicaid. Now some stress could be relieved. I was paying almost $700.00 a month for just my medications and I needed a CT scan of my brain to ensure the clip had not moved. Two months after receiving my SSI payments I received my SSDI, which is the Disability Insurance. Now I was elated as this was much more money for me....it is based on your past earnings. Problem is on SSDI I now had to apply for my Medicaid through the state of Florida. Have you ever had the experience of calling an agency and spending at least ten minutes on the phone just working your way through the proper numbers to push to reach a representative? Just when you think you are at the end of your journey a recording comes on "Sorry we are all busy at this time, please call back later." CLICK. After months of paperwork, phone calls, and in person visits, I was denied full Medicaid but qualified for their Medically Needy program. I had to meet my share of cost per month of medical bills before they would pay for more medical issues, prescriptions, etc. Needless to say my share of cost is $210.00 less a month than my income from disability and my mortgage payment was eating up 9/10's of my Disability payment. Should I also tell you that during this time Karen and I applied for a loan modification since the government came out with that program and I could not afford my current mortgage payment. I had moved to Florida for work and bought my house at the height of the boom down here so I am also upside down grossly. After months of calls to my bank they finally admitted they lost all of my personal financial paperwork we had faxed them. I had faxed it to them twice. I was not looking for a free ride....just some reasonable assistance that could hold me over. I also wanted help to continue my therapy.
It is crucial the therapy continues right after the brain injury. I realize I sound bitchy in this chapter and I truly apologize for that. I have one last topic for this chapter and then I will move on.

Karen and I were told to contact the Brain Injury Association of

Florida for help. We did, however they told us that they could not help me because my traumatic injury was not caused by an outside force such as a car accident, a fall, bullet or concussion. They could only help people with that type of injury. Never mind the fact that I had an aneurysm in my brain rupture causing a severe bleed surrounding my brain, that a coil shot through the aneurysm and lodged in my frontal lobe. Isn't that a form of projectile? Again I apologize for sounding sarcastic but an injury to the brain is an injury to the brain. I suffer from short term memory loss, can't concentrate, can't think or reason the way I did before. My emotions go from one extreme to another. They call that pseudo bulbar affect. I have lost the peripheral vision in my right eye so I still do not feel comfortable trying to drive. As a dear, dear friend, Elaine, from my support group said one day, "I am me but I am not me." I knew exactly what she meant by that. I am Diane, still have my sense of humor, but things I was once good at I am not anymore or I can't even do. Do I dwell on that? No, I do not as I am alive and it is truly a miracle. I see every day as a gift. I appreciate everyone in my life and look forward to making new friends.

CHAPTER 8

As the time went by I started looking at Karen and realizing that she really truly still cares for me. She went through years of therapy to help her with some issues she had. I was starting to laugh with her, have fun, and enjoy every day. Karen needed to go back to NY but said she would and could come back if I needed her and I needed to have a friend come down for a few weeks if not longer. We had dated on and off for several years; it was a crazy relationship actually, not healthy for either of us. I called my friend every night to talk and since I wasn't working or anything I did not really have a lot to say. Anyway my friend wanted to come down and see me and help me. So we made the arrangements. She came down and as much as we tried we came down to the same problems we always had. After about a month we realized it was not working so I asked her to leave. I knew I could not live alone yet but I knew more that I shouldn't be in a relationship that isn't healthy for either of us. My brain could not handle any stress. I would figure out who could help me do certain things, my house would not sell in this market so I could not go back to NY. I talked to Karen on the phone and told her my friend was leaving and if she could, I would certainly love her to come back down here with me. I told her she did not have to but she insisted so I let her. She came back down and as fall grew closer to Christmas it was an excellent time. We both enjoyed the holiday and making our home look festive. So we spent time doing that, working with the Support Group, working on my cognizance skills, and I realized that I was falling in love all over again with her. I told myself, Diane, think this through. What will some friends and family members think? I then heard a little voice that said "Follow your heart-Be Happy." As my wise friend Carol told me once "The World spins around every day.....either you watch it go by or you jump on for the ride" I will always remember that line. I was given a second chance at life and I was going to enjoy every breathing moment, what happens to me financially happens. Speaking of Carol, she called me and said that she wanted to come and visit us. I was so excited but also was wondering what she would think of me. She drove down to Florida from NY with her boyfriend Bob and stayed for several days. Every time I tried to speak with her I stuttered awfully. She held my arm and said "My friend, it is okay if you stutter, maybe if you try to slow

down and not talk so fast it will help you."So right out of mouth I did something I hadn't done in years. I started singing a song with my own words. It went to the tune of "Feeling Groovy" Here it is:
Slow down you talk too fast,
ya gotta make the moment last.
Just settle down and talk more slowly,
Do, do do do do, talking groovy....
Lalalalalala...talking groovy.

Needless to say we started laughing hysterically which felt so good and normal. Years earlier I had written a song about Carol that went to the tune of The Beverly Hillbillies. I met Carol when I lived in Little Falls, NY. Carol and her husband Frank moved to Little Falls and purchased a large, four story brick building which sat next to the Erie Canal and Mohawk River. They opened the shop to sell their unique garden ironwork and rented spaces to other antique dealers. I loved to look at antiques so I was always in and out of their shop plus I used to walk Jalapeno along the path next to the canal so would pass by her shop almost daily. Carol and Frank were both very fun, outgoing people and I really got to know them while stopping in at the Piccolo Cafe which is near their shop. They would always sit at the same seats at the bar to have some drinks and dinner. One day all of that dramatically changed. I was walking pass her shop one day and saw some police standing on the other side of the road talking. When I came back from my walk I saw more police cars parked in Carol's lot. I walked inside to see what had happened and found out that Frank had been traveling with some iron pieces he had purchased in Texas. His trailer broke in Indianapolis so he had stopped at a motel for the night. Unbelievably the police had informed Carol that Frank had been murdered right outside of his motel room. Poor Carol was devastated, in shock and crying uncontrollably. It would be hard enough to hear that your husband was killed in a car accident but to have to be told that he was murdered with a knife? The next week was a total nightmare for Carol as all of the details were released and the difficulties she faced having Frank's body released back to NY. It turns out that Frank was actually a hero as he killed his attacker. His attacker was on the run from another state as he had just bludgeoned his parents to death. He probably thought that this old man was a good target. Little did the attacker know that Frank was a strong man and Frank managed to reenter his room to grab his gun from his suitcase. Carol stayed in Little Falls for months afterward but things were hard financially so she ended up selling her house and moving back to her family in western NY. Carol and I became close when she was readying her house to list for sale. I helped her pack, sell items, paint, whatever she needed to have done. We would have in depth conversations and realized that we had a lot in common.

CHAPTER 9

I began attending a Brain Injury Support Group which was located close to our home in hopes that Karen and I would gain some information to help us work through the system quicker. Bayfront has an excellent Support Group but it is too far to drive there plus it would be during rush hour. At our first meeting I met a great couple I had seen while at Bayfront. Ned (not real name) had suffered a severe brain injury after falling off a sixth floor balcony in 2006. He was readmitted while I was in the brain rehab ward due to a relapse he was suffering. His wife, Alice (great sense of humor, not real name) visited him daily. One night as they were sitting by the window in the hallway Alice said Hi to me and asked me to join them. I was more than happy to as they seemed like such a loving couple. This was a large turning point for me. As besides having friends to make the nights go faster I also learned a very important fact. I could have an ice cream when I wanted one. Every night Ned sat with Alice and ate a small container of ice cream. Well........BIG MISTAKE!! Every night after dinner I enjoyed my dish of chocolate ice cream. You know your life has changed when the highlight of your day is having some chocolate ice cream near a window looking out over the building next door. Problem is when I did finally go home I wanted to eat ice cream every night. (Something I never did before.) Do you know what happens when you stop walking your dog daily and eat ice cream every night? Yup, I became a little chunky. My body was not working at full speed anyway so a major lack of exercise and a new friend known as "Chocolate Brownie Delight" packed on the pounds. Within 3 months of being discharged from the hospital I had gained thirty pounds. Considering I have spent my entire life maintaining a flat stomach; having this giant bulge can be quite depressing. Needless to say I stopped eating ice cream every night. It has been almost two years since I came home and I am still overweight. Karen and I are now walking Jalapeno every day, I am trying to exercise when I remember, and I try to strengthen my back. I really feel once I whip my body back into shape my brain will speed up also. We attended several of the Support Group meetings and were very frustrated that we could not garner any information; it seemed like the same people talked over and over again. Alice had talked with some other people and decided to start a new Support Group which would have a mission of helping both survivors and caregivers. We started out with 3 survivors and their caregivers. Each week we added more people. Our support group has been excellent therapy for me as Karen is one of the facilitators and she has me explain some of the information she wants presented at a meeting. Since I begin stuttering when I talk and then start crying or laughing this has been excellent therapy for me. I remember the first time I started crying I looked around the room and almost everyone else was crying. I felt terrible that I had caused that to happen. I am totally comfortable with the people in our group so it is great practice. Our group is now just starting to go out in the community to volunteer our time to help with food drives, helping in the local parks and just getting our name out there. We are available to speak with families with any brain injured members to help them readjust to their lives. Our goal is to be a simple resource for families to know where to go for assistance...to save them time and frustration. We have made lasting friendships from this group and are continually looking forward to touching more people. I cannot fully explain the frustration I feel at times when my brain does not work as it once did so I feel so much better when I can relate to a new member and try to help and comfort them with what they are now facing. People look at me and don't realize I have daily challenges. I make a daily list of things I need to accomplish so that I can stay on track. Problem is something that should take 20 minutes can take me 3 hours as I start daydreaming and lose track of what I was doing. I know I frustrate Karen at times as she ends up picking up my slack around the house. I will see that the dishwasher is done and full of dishes but then walk away not thinking about emptying it. The two things do not correlate. Another issue I had which I had a difficult time dealing with was panic while shopping in a store with Karen. If she went in a different aisle my heart would start racing, tears would start flowing and I froze with fear. I could not help myself and yet in my brain I could not understand why I was acting this way. It was extremely embarrassing. The opposite of this behavior was the loud laughter exploding from me for absolutely no reason. At the check-out register I would have clerks ask me if I had started partying early that day. When we would go to a restaurant I would always use my cane even after I did not need it. Since I laughed real loud and wobbled when I walked if I did not have the cane people would think I was drunk. It was easier to have the cane then to try to explain my condition.

CHAPTER 10

I need to go back in time a little now as I forgot to write about our trip back home to see my family and friends in New York. A year after I left the hospital Karen and I planned to visit my family back in New York State. We were going to be there to celebrate my Dad's birthday and all of my sisters and brothers would be there. We planned on driving so we could take Jalapeno with us. Now I need to explain the major feat that Karen was tackling by driving me for three days in the car. I am terrible in the car. I am extremely nervous in traffic; hence I am usually saying "Watch out" or "Be careful". Karen definitely was taking on a challenge. Since I had not driven in over a year and I was used to always driving I was worse than any backseat driver could be and I was sitting in the front seat near the action. Karen wanted to inform my family about some of the changes they may see in me and that they were normal. No, I am not talking about my extra weight, but about some behaviors. I have PBA which is actually Pseudo Bulbar Affect. My frontal lobe of my brain suffered some damage and this causes extreme emotional changes. I can be talking seriously and suddenly burst into tears or laughter. I began stuttering and while talking I believe I realize it and then the emotions flow out. It is out of my control. I don't want anyone to get upset if they see me cry while stuttering so I usually end the conversation by saying "That's, that's, that's that's all fo, fo, fo, folks" So Karen sent this information before we visited.

It was so great to see my family. My brother John had purchased a restaurant with his wife the year before and they had our family gather there for my Dad's birthday. It was so much fun to see everyone and to reconnect with family. I am so happy and feel special to have lived to have this day. My Dad never noticed anything wrong with me which was great as I would not want him to worry. He has been living in a nursing home since my Mom passed away and he is in ill health and tired most of the time now.

We also made plans to visit my old friends from the town I lived in before moving to Florida in 2006. The town is called Little Falls which is quite the appropriate name, I may add. We made arrangements to visit my dear friend Robin and meet her at a local restaurant. Well what a surprise I had as Karen and I entered the restaurant. Sitting at a large table was Robin, Ann Marie and Kate. I was so flabbergasted and then Donna walked in also. It was such a wonderful surprise. All of my friends wanted me to give them details of what had happened to me. As I began to tell the story Ann Marie pulled out a pen and began writing on the napkins. She wanted to take notes so she could repeat my story to others. Needless to say this created more humor and we started laughing uncontrollably. When I first told them I would not go to the hospital without my underpants they all remembered the old saying their Moms also had. At once everyone said "never go anywhere with holey underpants. What if something happens to you......then you will be embarrassed seeing the Doctor with holey underpants on." So of course to not have any underpants on at all would be even worse. My friends all wanted details of my brain surgery so I had to explain how the surgeon cut across my scalp and peeled down my skin over my forehead. Ann Marie quickly shouted...."Oh You Can Do Face On, Face Off. How Cool." That became the running line of the night. We had such a fun time laughing and I truly realized what excellent friends I had. Ann Marie had an even better laugh when she learned I had a coil in my head. She said my emotions were like I had a slinky in my head....up, down, up down, up, down.

    While we were in New York the major task we needed to accomplish was to pack Karen's belongings so she could bring them down to my house. She lived near her family so we were able to visit her friends and relatives in between packing. I know there was not as much time as we should have had for Karen to see her family and friends. Packing was definitely a challenge as Karen took photographs all of her life and kept them in albums. You can only fit so many photo albums in a box that can be carried so we were flying through boxes. My beautiful niece, Rhonda offered to drive the U-Haul down for us as long as we got her a bus ticket back to North Carolina. We rented a U-Haul and Robin, Ann Marie and Rhonda came to help us pack up. Needless to say you could instantly see it was going to be a tight fit. We packed every single inch as tight as we could and yet still did not have all of the room we needed so Karen had to leave some of her things. That always bothered me as besides leaving her family she was leaving some possessions. Our car was packed to the gills and Jalapeno had a little hole for her bed but we did it.

CHAPTER 11

Well, I passed my two year anniversary since I suffered from my head trauma and here I am finally writing again. I asked Karen to please help me schedule two hours a day to sit and write my book. No excuses from me and no wandering off to think about doing something else. I have a very short attention span and this structure is important for my continuing recovery. Someone can discuss an event that took place years ago and I can remember some details but ask me if I took my morning medications and I just shrug and can't remember. I have to go look. Our brains are very complicated. Karen is also trying to teach me how she makes some of her crafts. I will sit and start to paint some boards that she needs to have done and a minute later I am staring into space. The sad thing is; if we could finish some of these wooden flags, plaques, and other items we could set up at one of the many Farmer's Markets they have down here to sell the items and earn some money.

It is a beautiful 85degree day today and we are at the beach with Kathy. We packed our lunch so could hang out a few hours to relax and enjoy the sights and sounds of the Gulf. Kathy couldn't wait to go into the water as she had just purchased a beach noodle. For those of you that do not know what that is I will explain. Kathy wishes so much she had come up with the idea and invented it. The noodle is just a long tube four to six feet long made of Styrofoam. It floats in the water so it is great for the ocean or a pool. Every store around us has them for sale. Kathy says she can hear the registers going kaching, kaching, kaching and sighs that she could be retired now. Poor Kathy works like crazy and misses her children and grandchildren. I know one of these days she will leave Florida to live closer to them. As much as I miss my family and friends I can't see us living in New York again. I would not be able to deal with the deep snow anymore. Actually I am going to think positive right now as what I would love to do is sell this book and make enough money to be able to have a small place in New York for summer and fall and then a place in Florida for winter. We don't need anything fancy;

just a place to call home for five to six months. (Winters in New York are quite long so that would be about the right amount of time to be away from the snow and bitter cold.)

I am going to confess right now. I have not written anything new in this book since the last line about winter. That was written about four months ago. I have however gone back and reworded some pages I had previously written so I guess that counts for something. I still do not drive, still stutter, however I no longer cry as much. I do laugh much more and it is loud. I will start laughing and don't know why which makes other people laugh and so it continues. We are visiting New York again in a week. Karen's son is getting married so he is flying us to Albany for the wedding. I truly thank him and his wife for this as it will enable us to see my family and friends also. I can't wait to go even though I did promise everyone that the next time they saw me I would have a book for them to read. Ah well, at least I am still trying. I can at least print off the pages I have written thus far. This way they can give me their thoughts on my project. Of course if they say it sucks I don't know what I will do. I wanted to be a stand-up comic when I was younger so maybe I could still do that......I could use cheat sheets to remember the jokes. There is another positive with this because if the audience does not laugh at least I will be laughing. Maybe that will be contagious and they will laugh at that.

CHAPTER 12

We made our trip up to New York. The wedding was absolutely beautiful, actually when someone asks me how it was I call it a Fairy Tale Wedding. Karen's son and his new wife are so happy they literally beam sunshine when they smile; which is constant. After the wedding we traveled to Syracuse to see some of my siblings and my Dad. It was hard to see my Dad at the nursing home. His health is failing and there isn't really anything they can do for him. The one thing that touched my heart is I asked him why he wasn't teasing me about blinking. My eyes used to flutter a lot and when I would visit my Dad he would stare at me and flutter his eyes. I told him I did not flutter anymore I just stutter and he said Ye,ye, ye ,ye, yes, I know. Thank God he still has his sense of humor. Seeing him and most of my siblings made me think of my Mom and I cried. Memories came flooding into my brain and I lost it. Unfortunately the visit was short as we had to move on. The next stop on the trip was to visit friends from Little Falls. The first night Robin had planned for us to eat at Arthur's in Dolgeville as it was 2 for 1 Burger night. Plus we had a blast there last year. The next day was the Beverage Trail around Cooperstown.

Ann Marie said that she and Donna were going to write notes during this visit so they can be entered into my book. The rest of the chapter consists of the conversations we had as noted by Ann Marie and Donna. They titled their notes as "Here We Go Again". I will do my best at writing everything they wrote on napkins:

At Arthur's for the evening. Diane shared her brother's secret restaurant recipe for maple butter dipping sauce to go with their sweet potato fries. OOPS. He told her not to tell anyone and she promised. This will soon be published in Diane's book.

Diane also shared a story about laughing so hard with a friend and both of them wet their pants. Bad enough to be over fifty but to have lost a lot of muscle control doesn't help. She should really wear a small pad if she is going to be with other people and laugh.

Discussed the Support Group brochure.

Trying to convince Diane and Karen into getting married tomorrow. David Taylor could perform the ceremony.

Still in discussion.

Still in discussion.

Hold that thought, still in discussion.

Diane said no as they would want family there to see.

No problem we can have a wedding and a reception tomorrow.

Diane wants to know if Donna is talking to herself.

Now let's play torture Diane and make her put the menus back in the holder....so not happening.

Christmas party at the Canal Side. Robin asked D if she remembered when Carol wanted to order the best champagne they had and her and Ann Marie were waving, no, no, no. Let's just get drinks. Robin said the champagne would have cost more than what we had to spend for dinner.

Started discussing TBI and what it stood for. Traumatic Brain Injury, or in Donna's case we call it TDB, totally dumb blonde. (Major laughter)

I've been switched seats so now I can hit Diane when she stutters. She is like the old phonographs; just hit it quick and they will keep on playing. Hit Diane and she goes to the next word.

Wow, now we have the bartender stuttering with the rest of us.

Diane has a serious story to tell us but she keeps laughing....and laughing. Can't get it out.

She was told by her friend Kathy that at the hospital they did not think she would make it through the first night.

In Diane's other life, she gave away a cat and after her divorce she kept her married name. She had so much happening in her life she didn't bother with all of the paperwork. It was only a last name. Well now she wants to change it back to her maiden name.

No more Farmville, been too busy.

Di gets the burger program at Arthur's.

Okay, time to order burgers.

Diane will soon be wearing Donna's hair. The fan next to us is blowing away Donna's hair.

Back to wedding talk.......hold that thought.

Karen does not know how to open the bathroom door. So get this one! The TDB is going to show her how.

Now Diane has gone to the bathroom....wonder if she is coming back. Yeah here she comes. Let the laughter begin.

Now we are trying to talk Diane into becoming a stand-up comic. She is showing her age as she stated she wanted to be one just like Totie Fields. (Whoever that may be)

Diane tried to explain who Totie was and next thing we are picking on Joan Rivers.

Diane just stated she was relieved to find a stall in the bathroom as she thought there was just a toilet with no lock on the door.

We have decided to remove the coil from Di's head as SSSHHH. It is made out of platinum. (Worth money)

Donna is being a really, really totally dumb blonde.

Debbie has arrived, now we play musical chairs. Maybe tomorrow we will play a Chinese Fire Drill?

Diane----No looking!

Debbie starts talking about her Microtel experience.

Diane loses her train of thought and we are back to discussing Pulaski.

Karen wants to re-visit the marriage talk. Diane she is hitting me.

It's an open heart conversation.

Diane can't remember eating hamburgers here before.

Now she is claiming she does.....Not one of us believe her.

Diane is adamant she does not wear depends.

She finds it difficult not to squirt sometimes.

I am bringing my tape recorder tomorrow.

I think Diane just insulted Karen—had to do with sleep apnea and how romantic the machine is.

Di is very concerned with her bedroom appearance having to wear that mask and tube thing---too ffing sexy.

Now we are talking about colonoscopies. This one is for you Karen.

No, no, no for Robin. Hell her Gramma was 84 when she finally saw a Doctor.

Do you hear Donna?

NEXT DAY>>>>>>>>>>Ann Marie is driving Robin's SUV to Cooperstown so Donna is taking notes.

Diane said that Karen's legs were so much skinnier than hers.

Next she asks if anyone else is hot, could the Air Conditioner go on now.

Diane says she remembers the Canal Days Parade after Robin brought it up.

Donna shares that Bank of America's stock plummeted due to so many home foreclosures. A subject very near and dear to Diane's heart.

A gold wagon just pulled in front of Ann Marie on the way to Rustic Ridge Winery. Diane laughs and tells Ann Marie to blow the horn and boy does she.

Passed gold wagon. Donna says there are kids up here on 4-

wheelers. Re snaps at TDB.

Hysterical laughter and loud. Diane forgot the depends pad that Re gave her last night. Karen not surprised.

Now Diane talking about Kathy's driving. She just had laser eye surgery so maybe she won't hit the curbs anymore. Diane said "! **********, wait until you get my age and squirt every time you laugh." Donna said she was already older as she was 60.

Ann Marie trying to figure out what turn to make for Rustic Ridge. Di is a backseat driver. Trys to explain if you can't figure out how to go south to turn map upside down.

AAHHH---Wine tasting at Rustic Ridge Winery. Ann Marie is right up there "helping" Rick, the owner pour the glasses.

Diane is still trying like hell to give us directions.

Time to leave....Diane bought some wine and took brochures for her family.

Will Rick go home and tell his wife about the five of us? Hartwick. Re is asking how she cuts over there. Robin and Diane looking at brochure map and Di says don't worry Re we will tell you where to go and how to do it.

Diane begins talking about two guys she met at the Jack Jackson dinners; she is positive they lived in Hartwick, then starts stuttering like crazy. Donna hits her.

Driving to the Bear Pond Winery Diane suddenly says "please stop I want to have a picture taken." Ann Marie asked of what and Diane said the sign up there. It was a Beaver and she said she collected them all of her life so she wants a picture. Out of the truck go Karen and Diane and Karen takes a picture of Diane pointing at the beaver. The sign was for a campground.

Driving along now a conversation regarding us taking a road trip to John's restaurant in Fulton. We would do that.

Almost to Bear Pond, Di says when we come down to visit them we will do a fun trip. Karen says Diane will need a 2 month notice so she can research coupons for Dolphin Trips or Kayaking. Diane said we need to take the Turbo Boat for the dolphin tour as it goes fast, attracts dolphins and serves beer.......not like the old folks little ferry boat.

Visit to Bear Pond Winery much more quiet than at Rustic Ridge. So back in the truck we go....

Now on the way to the Cooperstown Brewery. We start talking about being older and having the squirting problem. Robin moans "I never ever Man" TDB says "Really?" Diane is carrying on a conversation regarding how she made up songs when she was younger. Had to hit Diane as she is a couple of conversations behind.

Quick joke---How do you keep Diane busy? Answer is Give her a map so she won't look up.

Okay, now at the Cooperstown Brewery. Karen actually trying some beer....yuck she says it is too strong. We finish our samples and head back to truck as Re and Robin can't wait to get to Brewery Ommegang. As we continue in the truck Diane says she needs some food. She starts talking about a great little appetizer that her brother used to make. The simple recipe is: Spread Heluva Good Horseradish Cheese Spread on a cracker then drop on a teaspoon of strawberry or raspberry preserves, top with a slice of jalapeno pepper. Zap in the microwave for 10 seconds. Karen says sure she can remember this but ask her if she took her pills this morning.

Hey guess what? Alcohol is good for Diane, she hasn't stuttered in over an hour. Beer.

Arrive at Oomegang and get a snack for Diane. Yummy twice-friend french fries with different sauces. Now outside to the sampling. It is beautiful out with a breeze. Had some samples, lots of laughs and jump back into the truck. Heading into Cooperstown Diane sees a street named Beaver Street. Stop the truck. Diane has to jump out and have Karen take her picture. What is this? Is Diane doing a pole dance on the Beaver Street sign?

Ann Marie and Robin want to stop at a tavern in Cooperstown to play some darts. We stop to play a game of darts. Diane is worried about not having practiced in over a year, she used to be good. No problem she missed all three of her darts. Darts all over the floor. WTF? Donna wins the game!!!

Now time to head back to Little Falls as Robin made reservation for 8:30 at Canal Side Restaurant. Diane is having a Hot Flash and Robin is freezing. Now a discussion on air conditioning. Diane said she has to wear jeans and a flannel shirt while riding in the car in Florida with her friend Elaine. Karen's phone rings. Their good friend Wayne, Elaine's husband had a stroke. Upset no one called to let them know. Wayne is doing great now so all Okay. Shortly after arriving at the restaurant Diane's old friend, Kim arrives to eat dinner with everyone. Another surprise for Diane. Hey let's call David as Karen and Diane could still get married tonight. It is early enough.

You may have noticed all the references to my trying to give directions. One skill that strangely was not affected by my brain aneurysm was my keen ability of looking at a map and being able to not only find my way, but also be able to picture any alternative routes. This not only amazes me it dumbfounds Karen and Kathy as they always nicknamed me Diane McNally as in the Rand McNally maps.

Chapter 13

Okay, I have to tell you....I am in big trouble now. I have not written anything in five months. It is
now January of 2012. How am I ever going to remember all of the things that have happened since then? Better go ask Karen about the last five months as I know I have had a life. I know I stutter more which is a story in itself. I am going to try to put everything in chronological order so here goes:

We came back from New York and worked like crazy making our recycled wood flags and signs. We wanted to be in a show before Christmas. Unfortunately every craft fair and farmers market we contacted has had a waiting list. In October we entered our first show. This was actually more of a dry run to see if we could load all of our crafts into our small Cobalt. Luckily the show provided tables as they would never have fit in the car. We didn't sell very much but we learned what we need to do. I have also made an interesting observation. When I talk to people I have discovered that when I start stuttering bad, women will say its okay, take your time to talk. A large proportion of the men will stutter back at me and laugh. If they keep it up I tell them that I suffered from a very large brain bleed and several strokes and then watch their faces drop.

Right after Thanksgiving Karen and I prepared to decorate our house for Christmas. Christmas was my Mom's favorite time of year. She not only made it special for her seven children she also kept a journal for years detailing each Christmas day. She wrote in this journal from her and my Dad's first Christmas together until my youngest sister was old enough to be on her own. Now let me explain the complexity of this project. I have collected Christmas items for years and so has Karen. We have enough Christmas collectibles to fill four houses and we live in a tiny 2 bedroom home. Needless to say Karen did most of the decorating as I would stop and then wander off into another room. I am still working on my concentration and attention span. After several days of intense work Karen had turned our little Florida house into a winter wonderland. Friends and neighbors could not believe what our house looked like. We also ended up with several large boxes of items that we could sell at our next Garage Sale.

Unfortunately about a week before Christmas my Dad took a turn for the worse in the nursing home. They had to admit him to the hospital as he was having an extremely difficult time trying to swallow and had developed another infection. My brothers and sisters living in NY had made plans to have him come to a Christmas party at my youngest sister's house on Christmas Eve day. That was not to happen. On Christmas day my family was called and told they might want to visit him that day. My Dad passed away on Christmas night and we have to believe that he was my mother's Christmas gift. I thought it was heart wrenching after my Mom passed away; now we had lost our Father also. My one sister summed up my feelings exactly. She said now we are orphans, grown-ups but orphans. This is another turning point in my life as my parents are no longer here and Karen and I both have friends with serious illnesses. I guess we are getting older and we should be keeping in better contact with our friends and families.

Karen and I were immediately trying to figure out how we could fly to NY for my Dad's funeral. Thankfully my youngest brother, John, offered to pay for the plane tickets and I could pay him back after the estate was settled. We felt so relieved we were able to be there. All of my brothers and sisters would have understood if we could not attend the funeral as they knew our circumstances. Karen and I felt it necessary that we reconnected with my family. It was not easy flights to New York and back. We arrived to the Tampa Airport on time and right before our flight was to depart they announced it would be delayed due to a mechanical problem. For people such as us with a connecting flight we could go to the gate to try and retain another flight out. I went to the gate while Karen tried calling the 800 number to change flights. Just as the agent was booking me different flights to Syracuse one of the attendants came up to her and said she could not do it as they had the part on hand and could repair the plane in about 15 minutes. So I went back to sit with Karen to sit and hear the announcement that a small motor that helped to control the tail function was faulty but they had a replacement motor which would take them a short while to replace. That was not a comforting feeling at all. We knew we had a two hour lay-over in Philadelphia so we would not miss our connection there to Syracuse. Well guess what? After about a half hour the voice once again came over the loudspeaker announcing that they had replaced the motor but unfortunately it did not work so the flight was now canceled. At this point there was a major rush up to the gate for everyone. Once again I went in the line and Karen called on the phone. I could feel myself starting to lose control but I was maintaining my composure.

I was now next in line and I looked over to see Karen waving at me. I quickly turned to the woman behind me and told her I had to go back to my friend for a minute would she please save my place in line. She kindly said yes so I hustled over to Karen. Karen told me she was in the process of booking the next flight to Philadelphia and the connection to Syracuse. I told her I would go back in line and if she arranged it first to wave for me to come. I went back to the line and thanked the woman that held my spot a million times. At least another ten minutes went by and I saw Karen waving me over. She had us scheduled on another flight but we had to go to a gate to obtain our boarding passes. Luckily they opened another gate so the line was only four people. We ran over to that line as the next plane would be boarding in twenty minutes. We patiently waited until we could not wait any longer. At that point I began to cry and I asked the couple in front of us if could just retrieve our boarding passes. Karen gave the agent our confirmation number and we received our boarding passes. We hustled to the new gate and boarded the plane. Right after the plane took off the pilot announced that there could be some heavy turbulence during the flight as we would be approaching a storm system in the Mid-Atlantic. We had been flying for over an hour and I was looking out the window and I saw a strange pattern in a field. I felt the plane turn and turn again and low and behold there was the same pattern. Again we turned and turned and the pattern once again appeared. I looked at Karen and I said we must be circling as I keep seeing the same field. Shortly thereafter the pilot announced that we may have noticed that he was circling. Unfortunately the whole Northeast corridor was backed up due to the storm and we would be landing for a while in Norfolk, VA. Karen and I looked at each other like "What do we do now?" Thankfully they allowed us to exit the airplane one at a time to use the airport's restrooms. When it came my turn I asked if Karen could please go with me. Right after we returned to our seats the pilot announced that we were allowed to take-off for Philadelphia. We did just that in within a half hour the turbulence became so bad that the plane was literally tipping side to side. My head hit the top of the window. The pilot announced that he was making the approach to Philadelphia. As I looked out the window I could see us going lower and lower over the tops of buildings and knew we were going to land shortly. As the plane was rocking every which way it suddenly went straight back up in the air. The pilot announced that he was going to do a NASCAR

and try again. We circled around and then re approached the landing
field. The plane rocked and rolled as the pilot managed to
touch the ground and bring us to a stop. At that point the plane
erupted in loud applause and you could hear sighs of relief. Karen
and I walked into the Airport and made our way to Terminal F. This
entailed going outside and riding a bus over to that gate. Well let me
tell you as we stepped outside to reach the bus the rain and wind
whipped us around like Dorothy's house in The Wizard of Oz. We
were cold and saturated. Once we arrived to Terminal F it was
announced that our flight to Syracuse had been canceled and we
needed to go to gate 36. We arrived there with dozens of people
ahead of us. Instead of standing in line Karen immediately dialed the
800 number on her cell again. She managed to obtain the last flight of
the night from Philly to Syracuse. It was to take-off in two hours so
we took our time going to the new gate. We sat there for over an hour
waiting for an agent to appear so we could obtain our new boarding
passes. After we received our passes we breathed a sigh of relief and
prayed to God that the wind would subside so we could continue to
Syracuse that night as the funeral
was the next morning. About fifteen minutes passed and the
announcement was made that our flight was going to be delayed as it
was late leaving Minnesota. At that point Karen asked me if I wanted
a beer and I eagerly answered yes. There was a bar right next to our
gate so we headed over there and had a cold, extra large beer. We
were so exhausted as it had been a long day and dragging our extra
luggage through the Philly Airport had also done us in. Finally at
9:30pm our plane arrived and we boarded and prayed we were now
heading to Syracuse. I called my sister, Ginnie and her partner,
Christina that we were due to arrive in Syracuse at 11pm as they were
picking us up. Now mind you we arrived at the Tampa Airport at
10am that morning. It had been one long day. Considering all we had
been through I was very proud of myself for not totally losing it. We
arrived in Syracuse on time and jumped in their car to return to their
house for the evening. The next morning we had to arise early so
could all get ready for the wake and then the funeral. We were
hustling so much that I had not had the time to let it sink in that I was
going to my father's funeral. Once we arrived at the funeral home I
started shaking; both because I was scared, nervous and cold. When I
entered and saw my Dad I lost it
at that point. We had the wake and funeral and when we arrived at the
cemetery the cold wind was blowing extremely hard. I was shivering

as I was no longer used to the cold weather. My two oldest sisters had me sit next to them and they held me to keep me warm. I will remember that forever. We stayed in New York for several days before returning to Florida. Of course the day before we were to leave they had a snowstorm start............no worries the one thing that Syracuse is proud of is their Airport never closes. As long as your plane is there it will take-off and that it did.   I was very sad to leave but knew I would not miss the cold, blowing snow.

Chapter 14

So now it is May 6th. I just celebrated three years since my brain aneurysm and here I am back at the book. We have been very busy with our Support Group and deep down inside I feel that God kept me alive to share more of myself with others. I know there is much more for me to do, to share. Karen and I also found an excellent church which we now attend every Sunday. They are open to everyone and they mean everyone. I have always believed in Jesus but did not go to church as they were too stuffy and that I am not, plus most of them think it is wrong that I am what I am. Not so at this church and what a refreshing, beautiful feeling it is to know you can worship and be who you really are. I am in my mid fifties now and I live with another woman who is my partner; I am not hiding that anymore. We have a lot to offer others and we are who we are. One of the things that started bothering me about our group was that we started out saying we were a brain trauma support group for everybody, young, old, gay, straight, veterans, etc. and we are here to help anyone who has suffered any kind of brain trauma. Well one of the members wanted the "gay" part removed. I wanted to stand up that night and say "Does that mean that Karen and I cannot come here anymore?" Needless to say I did not say anything. Since then I find myself not as excited about the group as I once was. How can you be supportive but limit who you will support? That to me is like going to buy a bra but the support wire is only on one side so take your pick. Do you want to droop on the left or the right?

     We have been very; very busy building our flags as we have secured a booth at Gay Pride in St. Petersburg on June 30th. Last year between 80,000 to 90,000 people attended so that is quite a crowd to sell to. I have excellent intentions of assisting Karen for hours every day. Somehow, someway, time flies by and I have accomplished very little. Karen has been working extremely hard and she was feeling ill quite a bit. She finally broke down and went to our Doctor. It turns out that when Karen was sanding the old painted fencing she was exposing herself to arsenic. She was poisoning herself.   Now the sanding is all finished and we are just constantly painting the wood. We have had volunteers from our support group come over to our house to help us paint. The help has been so welcomed plus we have mini therapy sessions with each other. I know I am not the only one benefiting from the concentration and eye-hand coordination. On the first day that we had a mother and father and their son who suffered a severe brain injury in a car accident seventeen years ago there was a humorous moment. The father looked at the green and red slats they were painting and I was painting purple slats he asked what type of flag we were painting as he knew Mexico had green and red but he could not picture purple. I told him we would be painting three other colors as we were painting Pride Flags for our show. That quickly broke the ice and we had a great afternoon. They came the next day also and the Father asked me if I would get offended if he told a joke about someone who stuttered. I asked him to please tell it as I had heard a great one a few months ago and I could not remember how it went. Well here is the joke. "There was a man who needed a job and he went to apply for a position as a Bible salesman. At the interview he stuttered like crazy. The owner told him that he didn't think it was the right position for him. However week after week the man returned to the owner and said I, I know, know th th th th th that I ca ca ca ca ca can d d d d do itttttt. The owner was so impressed with the young man's determination that he hired him. The first week on the job the new salesman sold his quota of Bible's and the second week he asked for more and sold all of those. Within a month he had sold more Bible's than anyone in the company. The owner called him into his office and asked him how he was able to sell so many Bibles. The salesman said, iiiiittttt isssssssss rrrrreally sssssiimmmmmssimmsimple, I I I I tell tell tell tell tell tell th th th th th th them th th th th that they either bbb bbb bbb bbb bbbuy the Bible or I I I I I wil wil wil wil wil will m m m m m m make th th th th th them si si si si si si sit d d d d d down and lis lis lis lis lis listen to me me me me re re re re re re re read it to to th th th th th th them. Th Th Th Th Th Th Th Th They al al al al al al always b b b b b b b b buy the Bi Bi Bi Bi Bi Bible. It t t t t t t t t t is ea ea ea ea easy." Needless to say I burst out laughing. I try to slow down and breathe when I realize I am stuttering but that usually results in me laughing hysterically.

Chapter 15

We now have nine days left until Pride Fest. Are we ready? No. However we now have a vehicle that can carry our flags, canopy and tables. We have been trying to purchase a used SUV or small truck so we can carry our wares to shows but since our credit is in the toilet we haven't had any luck. I started looking at brand new Jeep Patriots online and saw they were a reasonably priced SUV. Something told me to go to a local Chrysler Jeep to inquire. Karen and I pulled into the dealership and a saleswoman instantly popped out of a side door. Karen and I introduced ourselves and told her we were interested in a new vehicle but we had to explain our financial situation first as we did not want to unnecessarily waste her time. She told us her name was Marcia and said she was pretty positive that they could work with us. Within an hour I believe we had met almost everyone who worked at the dealership as Marcia had me laughing so hard that I was echoing throughout the whole building. It took just two days and there we were driving away in a new Jeep Patriot and leaving our Cobalt behind. I was excited also as the Jeep sits higher than our car did and has excellent visibility so I could try driving again. I also find it interesting that we craft Patriotic flags and that we purchased a red Patriot. I guess some things are meant to happen.

Well we did it. We managed to finish all of the flags and signs in time for the event. We crammed everything we could into our Jeep the night before the fest as we had to leave the house by 7:00am. That was a challenge in itself for me as I am used to sleeping until I fully wake up. For years I was always up and out of bed by 6:00am at the latest. On work days I wanted some time to myself before I ran to work and on days off I wanted to maximize the daylight hours. It took us two hours to set up so we missed seeing the bulk of the parade. Poor Karen had to lift more than she should have had to. She has bad knees and a back problem and I have lost most of my strength so I don't carry my fair share. By the time we were merchandised I was exhausted and frazzled but I put on my smiley face and hoped for crowds of people. The temperature and the crowd increased dramatically rather quickly. I wish I had a dollar for every person who said how wonderful our flags were but they would come back as they had a beer in one hand and a bag of free merchandise and brochures in the other hand. I positioned myself outside the front of our canopy so I could greet people. Occasionally we would have a customer actually buy something and our adrenaline would start pumping again. For the bulk of the day we just watched masses of wet, sweaty people walk by with beers in their hands. Finally an hour before we were to close a gentleman bought one of our large Pride Plaques. He wanted it for his house but didn't want to carry it around all day so he waited until he was ready to go home. He was our last customer of the day. Needless to say we didn't bring in enough money to even cover the cost of renting the space for the day but we definitely learned how to set up and tear down. We tried to look at the positive side of standing in 98degree heat all day.

It as after this debacle that we decided to focus on smaller events where the main focus was vendors selling their merchandise. This actually turned into an excellent thing as we met some wonderful people along the way.

CHAPTER 16

I have decided at this point in time in my writing that I am not going to try to do it chronologically anymore. I can't remember now what happened when. What I do know is that I have been on an amazing journey since my brain trauma. God has told me that I am here to spread joy to people's lives and help others as much as I can. My uncontrollable laughter makes other people smile and laugh. For some for maybe one minute they can slow down and enjoy part of their day. We have spent a lot of time with people who have recovered from a serious injury or disease and I am now learning something new. We met a wonderful couple, Myra and Ann, last year that have just the opposite scenario. Ann has been battling pancreatic cancer for two years. Already she has beaten the odds and is still fighting for her life. I am used to helping to support a person who has survived and is living with medical issues not someone who is facing a disease that is terminal. Ann has chemo therapy every other week.

The week she has her chemo she is so sick she is stuck in her bed. On her off weeks she tries to cram as much living as she possibly can into each and every day. Obviously it is difficult for Ann to deal with her illness and for Myra to watch her partner have to endure this plus the very strong possibility that Ann won't be with her as long as she thought. One of these days I need to sit with them individually to ask them how they truly feel. It seems like such a sensitive subject that we don't really talk about it. I believe it is time to do just that as they can teach me more about life and living.

Another large addition to our life is a wonderful woman named Jan France. She started a non-profit organization fifteen years ago called America's Disaster Relief. It is my love of food that gave us the opportunity to meet. On the first Friday of every month we became vendors in Largo. The first month directly across from us was a bright red tamale kitchen. Of course I had to go over to see what Mexican food they had. I ordered one of their burritos which weighed about five pounds. It was absolutely delicious. As I was waiting for my order I was looking at pictures of natural disasters posted on the wagon. I did not understand why they were there. All I know is Jan waited on me and she was the most wonderful woman to talk to. The following month they were again set up across from us. Karen and I found out that the tamale kitchen is used for two things. One is to raise money to buy items needed to assist at natural disasters. The kitchen is also towed to natural disaster areas where they can feed hot meals to people for free. Jan was actively in need of donations of blankets and warm clothing to go to NY and NJ to help survivors of Super Storm Sandy. After hearing Jan's story Karen and I wanted to assist her. We printed flyers of the needed items and walked in our neighborhood asking for any donations. We put a large tote on our porch for drop-offs. It is amazing what we collected in one week. We made arrangements with Jan to meet at her storage unit. Unfortunately she had not collected even close to what she needed for her trip north but we separated and boxed clothing, bedding and Christmas toys for the trip north Christmas week. Even though she did not have the money needed to buy gasoline for their trip up and back she was determined to make the trip the following week. Jan's favorite expression is "If plan A does not work then there are 25 more letters."

Needless to say at the last minute Jan secured gas cards and had arrangements to pick up more donations along the way. Once she arrived to New York she had many requests from communities. She not only distributed the donations she also helped redistribute water and supplies that some communities had an abundance of while others were in desperate need. America's Disaster Relief is a second responder. They arrive after the Red Cross and others have left areas to continue helping survivors. After spending nights of sleeping on church pews a wonderful benefactor provided them a night at a motel on Christmas Eve. This was a much appreciated treat. Jan continues to do her charitable work as unfortunately there are and always will be some kind of disaster; be it hurricanes, floods, tornadoes, fires. We plan on helping her as much as we are able to.

I am also extremely grateful to Dick Wood and Klaus Kokott for helping me ease into some kind of work life. They have given me some tedious data inputting work on the computer for their recruiting firm. They need it done but they could have hired someone who could do it faster. They both told me to work at my own pace which is excellent as some days I worked for an hour or two at the most and other days I may not do anything with it. I need this structure as I lack that still. As much as I loved working with people every day I can't picture myself at a work site. If I wanted to leave as I became overwhelmed I would not be able to do so. I kept track of the hours I worked on this project. It took me a total of fourteen hours to finish and that was stretched out over a two week period. So, as you can see, they have patience. Thank you gentlemen for helping me gain some confidence back.

Chapter 17

Alright, I am definitely tired of people asking me the same question over and over again "Have you finished your book yet?" I have to sheepishly respond, "No, I have not." Believe me I wish I could answer "YES, I HAVE!" Ah well that is one of the problems I have continued to struggle with. Every day I am busy but I don't know where the time went. I have now passed the four year mark that my brain aneurysm burst. It amazes me how fast the time flies by.

So, I have decided to put this book to bed. In the last four years I have learned many things. The first is that life can be short so love and enjoy your friends and family. Each day is truly a gift and should not be taken for granted. I now have a deeper faith. Some people do not want me to "talk religion". That; I say is their problem. I do not talk about religion, I talk about God and how blessed I am to be alive. I was already blessed in my life with a very contagious, boisterous laugh and I have not lost that. It still amazes me as once I start laughing I find others joining in so I am able to use that to spread some joy to others. When I almost crossed over and my mother told me it was not my time yet I knew that I am still here for a reason.....help others as much as I possibly can? I have been trying to do just that. My dream has been to write this book, have it be successful and touch others who have struggled with a brain injury. It would also enable me to continue with my volunteering efforts. I would love to appear on the Ellen DeGeneres show. Her quick sense of humor and timing makes me laugh hysterically. I have always admired the openness of her lifestyle. For so many years I hid that I was a lesbian. I will not do that anymore. I am who I am and Karen and I will be who we are. If I want to hold her hand while eating at a restaurant or sitting at the beach I will.

The Supreme Court right now is ruling on the constitutionality of "Gay Marriage". The majority of our country believes it should be legalized. Why not? There is no doubt in my mind that every adult has someone in their family or group of friends that is gay. In my family alone I have a lesbian sister, two nieces, a cousin and an aunt who unfortunately has passed on. "We are everywhere" and that is just one family.

The one very important subject I have avoided while writing my story is how I really feel. I still have not been able to accept how different my brain works. I know that Karen is extremely frustrated at times over some of the things I forget to do and especially when I forget what she talked to me about. In the past we had shared both working and living together so she knows more than anyone what "Diane" was really like. I was extremely organized, finished what I started, and balanced my work with my personal time. I find myself saying "I am sorry, I forgot" at least twenty times a day. I know it is wearing a little thin. I find myself going into the bedroom and crying out of frustration. I don't want Karen picking up after me like I am a little kid. After I release all of this emotion I sit back and tell myself to stop it. I am alive, I can talk and walk and have a wonderful family and friends. I am the way I am and I will accept this. This book is a perfect illustration of my lack of concentration. When I began writing my story I was so excited to share my miraculous story of coming back from the brink of death. I told everyone I knew I was writing a book called "Not without my underpants." I believe seeing my mother, hugging her and knowing she is in a beautiful place is a story I should share with others.   It has only taken me four years to finally finish my story. Whether it is a good read or not really doesn't matter as I actually finished what I started.

So to wrap this up I will leave everyone with a few words of advice:

Do not stress over your job; find something about it that gives you joy, or find another job.

Do not hide who you really are as every single person is unique.

If someone tells you they almost crossed over, believe them as it just may be true.

Heed your mother's words of wisdom. You may never know when you wished you had not left home without underwear on or lazily put on holey underpants.   Our Moms gave us so much to think about when we were growing up. Remember don't step on a sidewalk's crack or you will break your mother's back. As a child you can't wear a hat or you will go bald. Never swallow your gum as you will never be able to poop again. I remembered the first time I swallowed my gum I was scared all night that I would have a problem and have to confess. I thank God everyday that I listened to my Mom and stopped crossing my eyes. If they really stuck that way what would I have done?